THE
SACRED
CHALICE

THE SACRED CHALICE

WOMEN OF THE BIBLE
*The Inner Spiritual and Psychological
Meaning of Their Stories*

Andrew Cort

2013

SPIRITUALITY RELIGION MYTHOLOGY PHILOSOPHY

ISBN-13:   978-1492134855
ISBN-10:   1492134856

PRINTED IN THE UNITED STATES OF AMERICA

ALSO BY ANDREW CORT

The Door is Open
*The 7 Steps of Spiritual Awakening that Western
Scripture and Mythology Have Been Trying to Tell Us
All Along*

Symbols, Meaning, and the Sacred Quest
*Spiritual Awakening in Jewish, Christian
and Islamic Stories*

Love, Wisdom, and God
The Longing of the Western Soul

The American Psyche in Search of its Soul
Freedom, Equality, and the Restoration of Meaning

From Joshua to Jesus
*A Brief Chronicle of the Kings, Empires, Legends and
Ideas, that Paved the Way to Bethlehem*

The Song of Songs
A Lovers' Poetic Dialogue

Our Healing Birthright
Taking Responsibility for Ourselves and Our Planet

For Our Sons and Daughters

A Note Regarding Scriptural Quotations:

Lengthy quotations from Scriptures are generally italicized *and* centered on the page. For example:

> *The waters were split, and the Israelites went into the sea*
> *on dry ground, the waters forming a wall for them*
> *on their right and on their left. (Exod.14:21-22)*

(My own paraphrasings of biblical stories or extra-biblical legends are *not* centered on the page.)

Unless otherwise specified by a separate footnote:

1) Quotations from the Hebrew Bible are from the Jewish Publication Society Tanakh Translation.
2) Quotations from the New Testament are from the New Revised Standard Version.

Brief quotations, such as short sentences or parts of sentences that are discussed within the body of the text, are not usually individually cited, but can easily be found in the Scriptures close to the longer quotations that *are* cited and are centered on the page as described above. This avoids the distraction of excessive citations cluttering the book.

8

TABLE OF CONTENTS

INTRODUCTION

This is a book about the remarkable female characters in the Bible *and what each woman represents within our soul.* We won't be talking about their stories as 'literal history', and for the most part we won't be talking about them in terms of the social or ethical lessons they may contain. We'll be talking about their *inner psychological meaning.* We'll be taking the point of view that the Bible can be read as an allegorical, mythological, description – *a symbolic 'Instruction Manual'* – for the inner work the soul must do to rise from this lowly material state of being to a state of spiritual enlightenment. And we will see that at every step along this path the help of the Feminine side of life is required.

Among contemporary people, myths tend to be dismissed as childish fantasies or the unscientific gropings of primitive minds. This is why followers of western religions have typically insisted that their scriptures are not myths at all, but must be taken as literally true. This, however, merely weakens the effectiveness and power of religions, rendering them spiritually useless, often rather foolish, as well as socially dangerous. But the mythological vision of the world has always been, and still remains, a crucial way of experiencing and understanding reality. This is *not* because myths explain confusing historical events or strange natural phenomena. It's because myths reflect our deepest psychological and spiritual truths. They bypass the censoring mechanism of our mundane Reason and open the heart and mind to higher dimensions of consciousness, levels of being far above our everyday affairs.

On the one hand, human beings possess all the essential characteristics of minerals, plants, and animals. And yet, at the same time, unlike these lower forms, we can also be open to levels of reality that transcend the visible world. A human being, standing at the *center* of the creation, is thus potentially capable of intuiting meaning, truth, goodness, and divinity. This is the quintessential human quality. This is what makes a human being human. To deny this, robs us of our heritage and reduces us to nothing. When we shut the door on transcendence, we cut off any light from that world that might have illuminated this one, leaving us in darkness, leaving us with nothing but a dead world where scientists are merely performing an autopsy.

When read symbolically, the Bible tells the story of the soul's Descent from Heaven to Earth (what the ancient Greeks called the 'Lesser Mysteries') and then it gives instructions for returning 'home' (the 'Greater Mysteries'). Words like 'ascent' and 'descent', of course, are only a way of talking: what is being spoken of is *not* a change of external *location*, but a change of internal *condition*. This Sacred Heroic Quest to return 'home', to recover what we've 'lost' and return to communion with the Divine, has been called by many names: "The Return to the Promised Land", "The Quest of the Holy Grail", "Muhammad's Journey to the Seven Heavens", "Persephone's Return to Olympus", as well as many other names from all around the world. The different ways that these stories are told attests to the marvelous range of the human imagination, but the commonality of method and purpose that *unites* these stories is infinitely more striking than any of the differences – *they all tell the same inner story*, for we are all children of the same God, in the same boat, on the same path to the same destination. As the great poet Rumi has said:

If people but knew their own religion . . .
how tolerant they would become.
And how free from any grudge,
against the religion of others!

In the very first sentence of the Bible the One becomes Two: God, the One, creates Heaven and Earth. 'Heaven' represents God's Male aspect, and 'Earth' represents God's

Female aspect. We will see that throughout every step of the soul's descent and return there will *always* be a Feminine aspect as well as a Masculine aspect.

The Creation sequence *ends* the very same way it began: the One becomes Two. In this case, an androgynous 'earth creature' is divided into Adam-the-Male and Eve-the-Female. (We'll talk more about Adam and Eve in a moment.)

Most of *Genesis* then covers the story beginning with Abraham, who talks to God in the 'Promised Land', followed by the sequential stories of his children, grandchildren and descendants, ending in a state of slavery in Egypt. This entire story, when taken symbolically, represents the preparation of an *individual soul* which comes from a state of communion with God (Abraham and Sarah in Canaan) and descends, level by level, into the experience of material life in which we find ourselves here and now. Plato would call this "entombment in matter". The Hebrew Bible calls it "enslavement in Egypt". These are the *Lesser* Mysteries.

'Egypt', of course, does *not* mean a literal 'place over there', and the 'enslavement' is *not* 'something that happened to other people a long time ago'. In the Hebrew Bible, 'Egypt' is a symbol for *our* lives, *right now*. We are *all* "the children of Israel enslaved in Egypt". *We* must find our way home.

The rest of the Torah, and through the Book of Joshua, consists of the *Greater* Mysteries: Moses leads the Israelites from Egypt back to the Promised Land. That is, he guides our soul *from materialistic slavery to spiritual enlightenment.*

At every step along the path there is a necessary Feminine Principle as well as a Masculine Principle: e.g., Abraham *and Sarah*, Isaac *and Rebecca*, Moses *and Miriam*, Joshua *and Rahab*, and in the New Testament version, Jesus *and Mary*. This is absolutely critical to the soul's journey. In fact, we are going to see that without the help of the Sacred Feminine, attaining enlightenment is impossible! Without her, *all spiritual evolution is impossible*! She is the *key* to Creation and Return.

EVE

(The 'Rib')

Let's talk about Eve. First, we'll discuss the 'Rib', then we'll talk about the 'Fall'. The biblical story of Adam and Eve is the foundational story of our western civilization, and it has been horribly and tragically misinterpreted.

To begin with, the Hebrew word that is translated as 'Adam' is actually a *gender-neutral* word that means 'a creature of earth'. In other words, 'Adam' was initially created neither Male nor Female!

The creature was placed in the Garden and given only one restriction – not to eat of the Tree of Knowledge of Good and Evil. Adam lived a quiet, comfortable, rather unexciting life in the Garden, tending the flora and distributing names to the animals. But God saw that Adam was alone with no emotional life, no struggle, no tension. So God decided to put Adam to sleep and separate it into Male and Female in order to provide an emotionally meaningful life for humanity.

The Hebrew word *tsela* appears many times in the Bible. With one exception it is translated as 'side', typically referring to the side walls of important structures such as the Tabernacle. On one occasion only, here in *Genesis*, *tsela* has been translated as 'rib'.

This unique translation has had devastating, horribly destructive repercussions.

But if we give the word the same meaning that it has on *every other occasion*, the story makes more sense. God took *one side* of the composite creature and out of this he made Eve, the woman, and the *other side* became Adam, the man – *where neither had existed before*. The 'One' has become 'Two', and there is nothing in this description, absolutely nothing, to indicate anything but perfect equality.

The isolation of one human creature can now be replaced with a new form of wholeness that is attainable through erotic longing and love between two individuals.

One possible reason for the early translator's choice of the word 'rib' in this one place is that by removing a rib, God revealed the Heart of the creature, analogous to opening Pandora's box, thus bringing emotions (which are universally symbolized by the Feminine) into the realm of human life. Like Pandora's story, this is where pain and difficulty enter the world, *but also joy and meaning*, and only then do mortal beings become moral beings with the ability to make choices and mistakes, and thus to grow and evolve.

Even if we retain the word 'rib' as the translation of *tsela,* we see that this rib did *not* come from a previously created male, thereby suggesting some sort of primacy for the 'man'. On the contrary, the rib came from a previously created earth creature of no gender. And in fact, the Woman was created first!

EVE

(The 'Fall')

Later in the story of Eden, Adam and Eve are out and about and the serpent asks Eve if God has given any restrictions on what they can eat in the Garden. She says that God said they can eat of any of the trees except the Tree of Knowledge of Good and Evil: "Ye shall not eat of it, neither shall ye touch it, lest ye die." The serpent responds that "Ye shall not surely die: For God doth know that in the day ye eat thereof, then your eyes shall be opened, and ye shall be as gods, knowing good and evil."

Throughout western history, this advice from the serpent has been roundly condemned. But is it 'evil' to try to 'be like God'? Later on, in *Exodus,* God insists, "You shall be holy, because I, the Lord your God, am holy." So evidently we *can* be 'like God', at least in some respects: in fact, it is evidently our moral and spiritual obligation to *try.* So is it 'evil' to 'open one's eyes', to know the difference between Good and Evil? This can hardly be so. Understanding what is good and right, being moral and righteous, opening the 'eye of the soul' and perceiving the Truth – these are *precisely the initial goals of spiritual development.* It appears that the serpent's advice, in and of itself, was sound.

Of course, God did give a direct instruction not to eat of the tree, so traditionally we are told that *disobedience* was the key issue. But what a peculiar command this was! Do not open your eyes to the truth, do not understand the difference between right and wrong. What sort of God would ever demand such a thing? Could it be, as some have suggested, that this knowledge was forbidden on pain of death because God feared that human beings, acquiring the knowledge of good and evil, might become too like Him, too powerful, and endanger His supremacy? Is God paranoid?

Let's look again at what happened:

"When the woman saw that the tree was good for food,
and that it was pleasant to the eyes, and a tree to
be desired to make one wise, she took of the fruit
thereof, and did eat, and gave also unto her
husband with her; and he did eat."

Notice that Adam's behavior in this story is *completely passive*. Throughout the scene, he is "with her" but silent. The Serpent and Eve have their discussion, she decides to eat the fruit, she gives some to Adam, and he eats it too. And that's it! *The story doesn't say that Eve tempted him*, and nothing in the narration or in his silence suggests that she did. There's no indication that he's reluctant to eat the fruit, that his better judgment is overwhelmed by treachery, or even that he thinks about it at all. He says nothing and takes no initiative.

It is merely a passive act of acquiescence.

Socrates will later describe the human soul as composed of three parts – the Thoughts of the Mind, the Emotions of the Heart, and the Needs and Appetites of the Body. He shows how these parts are in a state of chaos and disorder, and he explains that to 'perfect one's soul' means that each of these parts must perform its proper function in a well-ordered harmony with the others.

The story of the Garden of Eden is a *parable of our inner life* and the need to evolve and *perfect our soul*. Adam represents the Mind, Eve represents the Heart, and the Serpent represents the Body's needs and appetites. (This use of males, females, and animals, to represent the three parts of every human soul, is customary in ancient myths and legends from all around the world.)

In their proper alignment, the Mind – our inner Wisdom – should be the *Active* principle that governs the soul. The Body should the *Passive* principle which supports the efforts of the Mind. And the Heart should be the

Reconciling principle that protects and nurtures the soul under the guidance of the Mind.

But what happened in the Garden of Eden is that this 'order' became inverted! The serpent (the *Body*) interfered, took the active lead, and persuaded Eve (the *Heart)* to go along with *its* wishes. Adam (the *Mind)*, silent and oblivious, passively joined in.

But Adam represents our Mind, and our Mind – not our bodily desires – is supposed to be the active decision-maker of the soul. *This* was the real 'sin' that occurred in the Garden of Eden, and that *re*curs within the soul of each one of us. This is the fundamental (i.e., *'original'*) sin – *the sin of an inverted soul.* Everything else is just a footnote. All the problems of our lives, all the problems of our world, begin here.

Our soul has been turned upside down, hypnotized by the world of matter, 'beguiled by the serpent'. It takes very little imagination to see that this allegory provides a complete and accurate description of our contemporary life – the garish pop culture, the insatiable greed, the relentless obscenity. Physical cravings and desires rule our lives, shape our culture, and drive the economy. Thus, the demanding Body has become the active force in our lives and is completely in charge. Wisdom has been belittled and 'deconstructed', and truth has been relativised, so the Mind has retreated into passivity. The Heart, mesmerized by all the gluttony and vulgarity that surround us, fawns over the cravings of the Body. We are upside-down, mad machines.

'Original Sin' is not "something an evil woman did a long time ago". On the contrary, *we are all committing this sin right now.* It is high time we stopped blaming 'Eve'!

When God returns to the Garden, His instructions are really quite simple. If the soul wants to evolve, the Serpent must crawl on its belly – in other words, the Body must be *Passive* and focus on the Earth. Adam, on the other hand, must "earn his bread through the sweat of his face" – that is, the Mind (the 'face') must become *Active*, make *efforts* ('sweat') and retake control of the soul. And Eve must "obey" her husband. But this grossly misunderstood and abused statement was *never* intended as a sexist or patriarchal command about marital life. It is an *inner symbol* which applies to us all, whether male or female, and it simply means that within the soul of *all* of us the Heart must be guided by the wisdom of the Mind, not the mundane cravings of the Body.

This advice is as valuable today as when it was first given. It is the necessary first step of spiritual growth.

SARAH

The story of the Garden of Eden is the conclusion of the Hebrew Bible's symbolic explanation of the creation of the world, ending with the creation of humanity. *Genesis* then tells another tale, a symbolic explanation of how a human soul descends from divinity to materiality, enters a body, and experiences the life of the world.

In the Jewish mystical tradition, the Kabbalah, Abraham and Sarah represent the attribute of Mercy, the highest human quality. The name, 'Abraham', means 'Compassionate Father', or 'Father of a Great Multitude'. Originally, Abraham was known as Abram, "High Father". His name is later changed – which symbolizes a great change in his level of being. For the same reason, the name of his wife – the feminine aspect – will also be changed from Sarai, "High Princess", to Sarah, "Princess of a Great Multitude".

Early in their story, there's a little story that reads like a preview of the soul's entire journey of Creation and Return. The couple descends from Canaan to Egypt because of a severe famine. In Egypt they meet Pharaoh, there's a plague, it's blamed on them, and in the end they load their wagons with gifts and riches from Egypt and return to Canaan. It's the entire Exodus story in a nutshell!

As they were entering Egypt, Abraham said to Sarah, "I know what a beautiful woman you are. If the Egyptians see you and think, 'She is his wife,' they will kill me and let you live. Please say that you are my sister, that it may go well with me because of you, and I may remain alive thanks to you." As he expected, the moment they entered Egypt some men saw her and were awestruck by her beauty. They brought news of her to Pharaoh himself, and she was taken to his house. And on account of her, her 'brother' Abraham was treated well by Pharaoh – who gave him gifts of gold, sheep, oxen, camels, and slaves.

But the Lord afflicted Pharaoh and his household
with mighty plagues on account of Sarah,
the wife of Abraham.
Pharaoh sent for Abraham and said,
"What is this you have done to me! Why did you
not tell me that she was your wife?"

At first glance, the couple's deceptive behavior seems a bit sleazy and Pharaoh comes off as an innocent victim. But let's look at what this story might mean. In the Kabbalah, the Sacred Feminine is described as the 'Vessel' that accepts and protects the 'seed', the Light, of the Sacred Masculine, like a chalice filled with wine. Later, she will pour forth the contents of the chalice, giving birth to all of Nature and life which she will nurture. It should go without saying that these two divine interdependent principles of Male and Female exist in a state of perfect equality.

Abraham and Sarah, who represent our highest level of consciousness, are wedded to each other in the appropriate balance and harmony of a perfected soul, with the enlightened Mind governing the Emotions, and the Emotions protecting the Mind. This is why Sarah does what is necessary to protect Abraham from Pharaoh – who represents the Ego, and is wrongly in control of the world represented by 'Egypt'. The Feminine always shelters and protects the Masculine – Rachel cares for Jacob, Miriam cares for Moses, Mary cares for Jesus, we will see this everywhere.

Sarah, the 'High Princess', is the archetypal essence of the Sacred Feminine (in Hebrew 'the *Shechinah*'), and as such she naturally glows with a heavenly beauty that ordinary people like Pharaoh have never witnessed before. The experience of the *Shechinah* always arouses desire, but desire exists in many forms – from the desires of a glutton to the desires of a saint. Abraham knows that the ego is always ready to take whatever it wants, satisfying its greed and lust, and believing without question that whatever it wants is its due: and it is quite willing to silence and destroy any higher representative of conscience (Light) that dares to suggest otherwise. This is Pharaoh's home turf where he is at his most powerful, so anyone challenging his authority would be in grave danger. Therefore, as the couple enters the realm of shadows, they devise a clever ruse so that Sarah can protect Abraham. By engaging in their deception, the beautiful Sarah easily distracts Pharaoh and ensures that he will not feel threatened by Abraham, thus carrying out the *Shechinah*'s role of protecting the Light of the Mind.

At that point, Pharaoh graciously turns over to Abraham much of the wealth of his kingdom, as a gift to his new queen's 'brother'. Then, while Pharaoh ignores him and concentrates on the beautiful Sarah, Abraham is able to mingle freely with the Egyptian people, experiencing all the aspects of the earthly realm.

And Sarah, the essence and power of the Feminine, was never in any real danger. The legends interpret her vast authority this way:

During the night, when Pharaoh was about to approach Sarah, an angel appeared armed with a stick, but only Sarah could see him. When Pharaoh tried to touch Sarah's shoe to remove it, the angel struck him on the hand with the stick. When he tried to touch her dress, a second blow followed. Whenever Pharaoh tried to do anything, the angel would look at Sarah and follow her command: she would slyly move her lips, instructing the angel either to 'wait' or to 'strike' as the case may be, thus toying with Pharaoh who spent the entire night suffering this humiliation (and, like most of our egos, refusing to quit despite accomplishing absolutely nothing).

When the sun came up, Pharaoh noticed signs of rot and deterioration all over his palace walls, on the furnishings, and even on the faces of his courtiers.

Horrified by this plague, he asked his priests what he must do. They determined that the cause of the affliction was Sarah, and she corroborated this, telling him that

23

Abraham was really her husband. Pharaoh then called for Abraham, appeased him with more riches, and sent the couple away as fast as possible.

In part, this is an allegory about the proper balance and alignment of the three parts of the soul. At issue is the appropriate 'marriage' of the Heart, and the appropriate purpose and ownership of material wealth. Pharaoh, the ego, has usurped the rulership of the soul here at the bottom of the Creation. He believes he can take whatever he wants, but he finds out otherwise: Sarah is not meant to be his wife – she is wedded to the Mind, to Abraham. And all that is truly good and valuable in the world does not belong to him. It belongs to the higher aspects of the soul which will raise everything up to be redeemed, as soon as material life has been fully experienced.

It is also noteworthy to see that in order to function successfully at this level of being, amongst folks like you and me, Abraham and Sarah are well aware they must employ cleverness and sometimes even trickery.

HAGAR

Despite several promises from God, Sarah was getting old and had still not had a child. She had an Egyptian servant named Hagar ['Stranger'], whom she had raised herself, and according to the accepted custom of the times she said to Abraham, "Consort with my maid; perhaps I shall have a son through her." According to Hebrew legends, Hagar was herself a princess, a daughter of Pharaoh, who had been given to Abraham and Sarah (see the previous story) to give her a better life.

So Abraham cohabited with Hagar – a union of the 'Above' (Canaan) and the 'Below' (Egypt) – and Hagar conceived. At first everyone was happy, but the pregnant Hagar soon began to treat the barren Sarah scornfully, reversing their roles and trying to increase her own importance, and Sarah complained to Abraham. He told her to do whatever she thought was right. She started treating Hagar harshly and Hagar ran away.

But God sent an angel to find her, and when the angel found her near a well (which always signifies a source of divine truth) he told her she must return home and put up with Sarah's treatment. But he promised her that God had heard her cries, and that through her son, who was to be named 'Ishmael', she would be the mother of a race of great warriors. Satisfied, Hagar responded joyfully, "The Lord has seen me!" She named the well 'Beer-lahai-roi' which means 'the well of the Living One who sees me", and then she returned to Sarah.

Thirteen years later, when Sarah was 99 years old, she gave birth to Isaac. Once again, a conflict arose between Hagar and Sarah. This time, Sarah became worried that Hagar's son Ishmael was going to share the inheritance she wanted exclusively for Isaac, so she told Abraham to cast them out! A distraught Abraham consulted with God, and God told him to obey Sarah but not to worry – God would take care of them and Ishmael would father a great nation.

Abraham then obeyed Sarah, he prepared water and bread for Hagar and the boy, and he sent them off. When the water ran out, Hagar burst into tears and walked away from Ishmael, for she could not bear to see him die. But God heard the boy, and He sent an angel to reassure them. "Come", he said to Hagar, "lift up the boy and hold him by the hand, for I will make a great nation of him."

Then God opened her eyes and she saw a well of water.
She went and filled the skin with water,
and let the boy drink.
God was with the boy and he grew up; he dwelt in the
wilderness and became a bowman. He lived in the
wilderness of Paran [which means 'Beauty' and 'Glory'].
(Gen.21.19-21)

So Ishmael, too, is to have a share in God's Covenant with Abraham. He, too, will give birth to a great nation. His father Abraham loved him – Hebrew legends confirm that Abraham loved his eldest son and visited him often during his long life – and when the time came for the boy to depart, he provided him with bread (spiritual sustenance) and water (spiritual truth). And when this ran out, God Himself appeared and gave him more: the Lord 'opened Hagar's eyes' – that is, He opened the Eye of her Soul, so that she could 'see' the Truth and convey it to her son. Ishmael, we are told, drank this 'water', and he went on to live in Beauty and Glory.

Why this conflict between Hagar and Sarah? Remember, this is a symbolic inner story. Women in the Bible represent Emotions. Both of these women are called 'Princesses', which means they certainly represent positive attributes. But Sarah represents emotions from the highest, most sacred part of the soul: Sarah comes from Canaan, the Promised Land. Hagar is a child of the Ego; she comes from biblical 'Egypt', which signifies the material level of the soul, the level of illusions. (Note that her son, Ishmael, is *of both* worlds.) Now Abraham is the Bible's great personification of Mercy and Loving-kindness, the highest qualities of a human being. But it is possible for loving-kindness to go too far, becoming undisciplined, and generous-to-a-fault. Sarah is once again protecting Abraham, this time from himself! Hagar and Ishmael represent very high level qualities, but they are *worldly* qualities, not spiritual qualities, and Abraham must not become too attached to them. Ishmael is a great and powerful warrior – a man of this world. The name 'Hagar' means 'stranger' – she is a stranger *in Canaan*, where it was completely inappropriate for her to try to reverse roles with Sarah and make herself superior. This, of course, is exactly what her father, the Ego, tried to do to Abraham when Abraham and Sarah were in his palace. So, Sarah is once again protecting Abraham and making sure that lower influences do not take advantage of him and usurp his authority.

REBECCA

Immediately after the famous episode of the near-sacrifice of Isaac, Sarah passed away. When the time of mourning was over, Abraham sent a servant to the land of his birth to find a wife for Isaac. When the servant arrived outside the city he stopped beside a well and prayed for a sign. Instantly the beautiful Rebecca appeared, who turned out to be the granddaughter of Abraham's brother, and who possessed a generous and loving nature much like Abraham himself. Rebecca agreed to return with Abraham's servant and marry Isaac.

Just as Rebecca reached the home of Abraham, the text says that "Isaac had just come back from the vicinity of Beer-lahai-roi" ('the well of the Living One who sees me', that was named years earlier by Hagar). It then says, "Isaac brought her into the tent of his mother Sarah, and he took Rebecca as his wife. Isaac loved her, and thus found comfort after his mother's death."

We are told very little else about Rebecca. But in the very next sentence the Bible says that Abraham also now remarried, this time to a woman named Keturah, and they had several children. Abraham lived to be 175 years old. When he died, Isaac and Ishmael buried him beside Sarah. After this, we are told, Isaac and Rebecca "settled near Beer-lahai-roi."

This perplexing medley of information begins to make sense when we learn from the Talmud that 'Keturah' was another name for Hagar. 'Keturah' means *perfumed*, and it is said in Hebrew tradition that Hagar was 'perfumed with good deeds.' Now notice that before Rebecca arrived, Isaac had been in Beer-lahai-roi, which *strongly suggests that he had been living with Hagar and his brother Ishmael.* Evidently, he and Ishmael brought Abraham and Hagar back together after Sarah's death. Abraham lived another thirty-seven years and had many more children, as did Ishmael, and this formerly divided family lived all together once again, everyone "alongside their kinsmen". When

Abraham passed away, Isaac and Ishmael brought him home and buried him with Sarah, and then Isaac returned to the family and "settled near Beer-lahai-roi."

Spiritually, the story reminds us that the various inner forces within the soul, no matter how divergent, can still reunite and work together in a state of harmony. On a psychological and family level, it suggests that it's never too late for broken families to come back to each other and heal their wounds. On a social and political level, given the immense importance of this particular family for all of western history, it clearly tells us that *since Isaac and Ishmael could reunite as brothers, there is no reason why their children, Jews and Muslims, cannot do the same.*

Isaac and Rebecca then had twin sons, Jacob and Esau. Esau grew into a fierce hunter. His temperament was much like his father, Isaac. Jacob was quiet and mild mannered, a gentle soul like his mother and his grandfather. According to the Kabbalah, the original divine plan was that the twins would share the responsibility as the next Patriarchs of Israel: Esau would be responsible for the nation's physical well-being. Jacob would be the priest, responsible for the nation's spiritual well-being. But Esau did not like responsibility. He was selfish and violent. This changed Jacob's destiny. By whatever means necessary, he would have to take Esau's job away from him, and balance both archetypes within himself.

The story of how Jacob took on both roles began when Esau came home hungry after a hunt and Jacob was cooking a stew. When Esau asked for some, Jacob said, "First sell me your Birthright," and Esau agreed. Shortly after this, Isaac, whose eyes were growing dim and knew he soon would die, told Esau to hunt some game and prepare a meal for him. Isaac would then give him his Blessing as the eldest son.

But Rebecca had been listening and she knew better, so as soon as Esau left she called Jacob and told him to disguise himself as Esau, bring Isaac a feast she would prepare, and take the blessing. The ruse worked, and Jacob now possessed Esau's Birthright *and* Blessing – he had thus taken on the responsibilities of both brothers. The journey forward of the soul could now continue, thanks to the cleverness and protection of Rebecca.

RACHEL AND LEAH

After stealing Esau's blessing, Jacob escaped his wrath by running away to Rebecca's brother, Laban. Rebecca covered for him by telling Isaac he went to seek a wife among his own people. Soon, Jacob came to a well and the beautiful Rachel appeared, just as Rebecca had appeared at the same well long before.

In Biblical symbolism, water represents a high level of divine truth, and a well signifies a source of this truth. When Abraham's servant came to the well it was open and accessible. But now, in the journey of descent, the soul is moving down into denser levels of materiality, so when Jacob came to the well he found it covered by an enormous stone: i.e., the divine truth was blocked by dense, heavy, matter. When Rachel came to water her father's flock, Jacob (who had come from 'Above') went up and rolled the stone off the mouth of the well. Jacob then kissed Rachel, and broke into tears. He had contacted the *Shechinah*, the Sacred Feminine, in Rachel, he recognized her immediately, and all the waters of divine love and sustenance began to flow down and "feed the flock".

Rachel took Jacob to her home, and soon thereafter Jacob asked Laban for her hand in marriage. Laban agreed. But Laban was a crook and a swindler. For a long time he'd been anxiously awaiting the day when Jacob would arrive – ever since the day when Abraham's servant had arrived with gold and jewels on behalf of Isaac. To Laban's great disappointment Jacob had no gifts to give, so the two men struck a deal: Jacob would work for Laban for seven years, and then he could take Rachel as his wife.

When the long-awaited day finally came, it turned out that Laban's wicked ways were just beginning. In the morning, after consummating his marriage, Jacob beheld his new wife and discovered it was Rachel's older sister, Leah! "What have you done", he demanded. "I was in your service for Rachel!" Laban replied, "It's not our practice to marry off the younger before the older." He then told Jacob that, if he would agree to continue working for another seven years, he could marry Rachel as well, immediately after the bridal week. Jacob agreed to these terms.

On one level, it appears that Jacob is getting back a bit of his own. After all the tricks that he pulled on his brother and father, he now must repay karma by being the object of his uncle's deceptions. But again, there's a deeper meaning to the story. The Kabbalah suggests that Rachel and Leah had *always* been betrothed to Jacob and Esau. Like their cousins, the sisters were different types. Leah was quiet and contemplative, the unworldly daughter who stayed at home. Rachel was the active daughter, who went into the fields to shepherd the flock. Rachel was of the earth, and she had a physical beauty that immediately attracted Jacob. But Leah was not of the earth. *Genesis* describes her as having "weak eyes". Symbolically this means that she did not see well into this world, for *she was always looking inward.* Leah was not pretty, but Leah had a beautiful soul.

The intended betrothals of Jacob and Esau with Rachel and Leah were a perfect matching, balancing, and completion of qualities. Esau, the man of action, would be united with Leah, the woman of contemplation. Jacob, the man of contemplation, would be united with Rachel, the woman of action. This was all part of the divine plan. But it all had to be changed, for Jacob was no longer just Jacob. Having acquired the birthright, the blessing, and in fact the entire archetype of Esau, Jacob was now both men. To complete the divine scheme, both women needed him equally, and he needed both of them equally.

Leah is the personification of 'Understanding' according to the Kabbalah, on a very high, sacred level. Rachel represents the physical manifestation: she is the *Shechinah* – the 'presence' of God in the tangible world. Jacob, having previously sealed together his brother's qualities with his own, now unites with these two feminine energies as well. Out of this extraordinary 4-way union will come the Twelve Tribes.

Leah and Rachel gave Jacob twelve sons and at least one daughter (some sources say 12 of each). The number Twelve is a symbol of abundance and multiplicity. It is formed by taking the sacred number Three (the symbol of the soul which exists between worlds) and multiplying it times the number Four (the symbol of material manifestation, the symbol of the body), so that together the Three and the Four generate Twelve. This is an image of the soul (Three) entering matter (Four), and awakening it to life, growth, and fruitfulness. This is why the ancients divided the vast planetary realm of heaven into Twelve Constellations, and why the Bible speaks of Twelve Patriarchs, Twelve Disciples, and tells us that when Jesus fed the multitudes with five loaves of bread, even the remaining *fragments* of the loaves, *"left by those who had eaten, filled twelve baskets."* Psychologically, the birth of Jacob's many children symbolizes the vast multitude of human qualities being brought down into the material world.

The Kabbalah tells a magical story about the birth of Dinah and Joseph. Leah was fruitful and had six sons. She also had two more sons through her handmaid. Rachel also had two sons through her handmaid. But Rachel herself had long been barren. Now Leah was pregnant again, and so, at last, was Rachel. Leah was carrying another boy, and Rachel was carrying a girl.

Leah felt compassion for her sister and prayed that Rachel might give birth to the son (so that Rachel would give posterity at least one of the prophesied twelve tribes) and she herself, after so many sons, would carry the daughter. God heard her prayer and switched the children in their wombs! Leah then gave birth to Dinah, and Rachel gave birth to Joseph.

In Scripture, the birth of a son represents a new spiritual attribute of the *Mind*, and the birth of a daughter represents a new spiritual attribute of the *Heart*. Some legends claim that eleven of Jacob's sons had twin sisters, feminine analogues of the masculine attributes of the brothers (there is even a corroborating line in *Genesis* that refers to "all the sons and daughters of Jacob"). Actually, what this story is really getting at is that the Patriarchs, like Adam when he first was created, and like *all* levels of Divinity prior to descending into the physical realm, are *both male and female*.

Only Joseph and Dinah were not born with twins. But the miraculous story of their birth shows how deeply they were connected, that they were *spiritual* twins. Together, these two children represent the male and female aspects of the human Soul that will soon cross into the material world. Fathered by both Jacob and 'Esau', nurtured in the wombs of both Rachel and Leah, these soul-partners bring *everything from the 'Above'* with them.

By the time of the births of Dinah and Joseph, the years of Jacob's servitude to Laban finally came to an end, and it was time to take his family and begin the journey down to the next stage of the Lesser Mysteries. But Laban did not want him to go, for he had grown very rich over the years due to Jacob's efforts. In addition, Laban was an idol-worshipper, he practiced a form of sorcery and fortune-telling with his idols, and these had warned him that if Jacob were to leave, Laban's wealth and abundance would go with him. (It must be noted here that although the Bible warns us against the use of magic, it doesn't say that magic doesn't work!)

Unbeknownst to Jacob, as the family was secretly preparing to leave, Rachel stole her father's idols so they could not warn him of Jacob's flight. But Laban's shepherds noticed that the well, which had flowed abundantly since Jacob's arrival, had inexplicably dried up. Laban immediately realized that Jacob must have departed, and he rushed off in pursuit. But God came to Laban in a dream and warned him not to try anything amiss with Jacob. So when he caught up with the family, he only demanded to know why Jacob had stolen his idols.

Jacob, unaware of what Rachel had done, found this accusation ridiculous, and he told Laban to go ahead and search everyone and everything, even adding, "anyone with whom you find your gods shall not remain alive!" Laban rummaged everywhere in search of his precious idols, but found nothing. When he entered Rachel's tent, she asked him to excuse her for not rising in greeting because, she said, "the period of women is upon me." He never knew that Rachel was sitting on the package of his idols.

And so, using all her cunning and wisdom, the *Shechinah* has transferred all of Laban's power to Jacob.

DINAH

During their travels, Jacob and his family came to the city of Shechem. Jacob bought some land from a man named Hamor, whose son's name was Shechem, like the town.

On one particular day, while Jacob's sons were out pasturing the flock, Hamor's son Shechem brought some of the young maidens of the land to sing and dance near the Israelite camp. Dinah, now a girl of about thirteen, went out to see them. Shechem took her and raped her.

Jacob heard that his daughter had been raped, but he held his tongue and did nothing until his sons returned home. In this symbolic moment Jacob ceases to act, giving deference to his sons. He has turned over the story to the next generation, the next level of Being – the Twelve Patriarchs.

When her brothers heard the news, they were outraged. But Hamor, the boy's father, tried to pacify them by saying that the boy *loved* Dinah, and wished to make things right by marrying her. Hamor then made a speech suggesting that the family should remain in his land, they could trade together, and all should intermarry. After all, this would be advantageous to everyone.

They couldn't do this, the brothers responded, because the men of Shechem were not circumcised. But if every male of the city would become circumcised, they said, "Then we will give our daughters to you and take your daughters to ourselves; and we will dwell among you and become one kindred."

The men of Shechem agreed to this condition and they all were immediately circumcised.

But three days later, when the pain of recovery was at its worst and these men were quite helpless, two of Dinah's brothers, Simeon and Levi, entered the city, took Dinah from Shechem's house, killed the boy and his father, and then killed all the males of the city. The other sons then came and plundered the city, taking all their wealth, their wives, and their children, because their sister Dinah had been defiled.

On the surface, the brothers' cruel and deceptive actions seem despicable. But this must not be taken literally. Dinah, the Feminine aspect of the soul, was ensnared and defiled by the lower forces of materiality (just as the Greek god Bacchus, who also represents the Soul, was ensnared and defiled by the Titans who were dwelling deep within the material earth: and just as the Titans were reduced to ashes by Zeus' thunderbolt, so the citizens of Shechem were completely destroyed by the sons of Jacob).

Here, in this internal story of the step-by-step preparation of a human being, this legend of a 'War in Heaven' (we are still above the physical earthly realm) represents the destruction of evil *within us*, evil arising from a lower plane represented by Hamor and his people who are trying to infest us, trying symbolically to 'intermarry': which means, mythologically, trying to mix lower emotions with higher emotions – a sin that the Bible calls 'Adultery'.

Hamor and Shechem are the 'Father' and 'Son' of the evil inclination of life. The 'Father' here is not generous like Abraham: he is greedy and grasping. The 'Son' here does not *sacrifice* himself: he *takes* for himself, he rapes and defiles what is holy and he has to be *killed*. The masses of townspeople, who did nothing to punish the boy, represent the *multiplicity* of all this negativity and evil – that is, all our greedy and malicious passions.

Before descending to the next level, the sons of Jacob (who symbolize our *high* spiritual attributes) must wreak terrible vengeance on all those who dared dishonor the Sacred Feminine, who dared defile the human Soul, who dared suggest a sinful union. To do this, they employed all the treacherousness of Laban and all the fierceness of Esau, qualities which they had now absorbed through Jacob.

They had also absorbed a spiritual generosity that was tempered by severity. So first they prepared the men of Shechem by circumcision, a ritual removal of their sinfulness. Then they completely annihilated this internal threat.

ZULEIKA AND ASENATH

We all know the story of how Joseph's brothers became jealous and angry and sold him as a slave to a caravan that was headed to Egypt. Joseph was sold to Potiphar, an official of Pharaoh's court. His very presence in Potiphar's home brought wealth and abundance to his master, just as Jacob's presence had brought wealth and abundance to Laban. Soon Potiphar put him completely in charge of his entire household.

The soul is now in 'Egypt'. It has reached the material world, the level of the Garden of Eden prior to the 'Fall' into slavery and illusion.

Like his mother Rachel, Joseph was extremely beautiful. Soon, Potiphar's wife, Zuleika, was overwhelmed with desire for him. Although he resisted her attempts to seduce him, she persisted, coaxing him day after day to make love to her. But he always refused, saying, "How could I do this most wicked thing, and sin before God?" Finally, angry and humiliated, Zuleika sought revenge. She told her husband the Hebrew slave had tried to seduce *her*. A furious Potiphar then had Joseph thrown into the royal dungeon. He remained there for ten years.

This is a story of how the soul *ought* to be balanced, how to *avoid* the Fall. This time, Zuleika represents the Heart and Joseph represents the Mind. Zuleika is completely under the spell of the physical appetites, and she wants to bring Joseph with her. This is not because she is evil (nor was Eve). It is because she sees that he is beautiful (like the fruit of the Tree), she recognizes that he is blessed with divine wisdom (like the fruit of the Tree). Plus, her idols have revealed that *her* posterity shall also be *his* posterity. This turns out to be true, though not in the way that she expected. But Joseph understands both on a literal level that it is a sin to sleep with a married woman, and more importantly, he understands on a symbolic level that he must not commit *inner* 'adultery' – he must not ally himself with lower forces.

43

Unlike Adam, Joseph is not passive, he does not sit silently and acquiesce. Joseph is *active*. He has already taken over complete control of the 'household': thereby, in terms of the symbolism, rendering the body *passive* which is as it should be. This time, when the Heart, beguiled by the physical, asks him to join her, he does not succumb. He does, however, pay a heavy price.

After 10 years Pharaoh released Joseph from prison when he heard about his ability to interpret dreams. Deeply impressed with Joseph's abilities, Pharaoh put him *in charge of the entire nation* and the preparations to store food to prevent famine. Pharaoh also arranged for him to be married, and his wife was to be none other than Asenath, the beautiful daughter of Potiphar and Zuleika!

Asenath gave Joseph two sons, Ephraim and Manasseh. And thus, Zuleika's idols were right, and her posterity was also Joseph's posterity!

However, some legends say that Asenath was the *adopted* daughter of Zuleika, and was actually the daughter of the rape of Dinah, Joseph's sister. And this union symbolizes the beginning of the necessary healing that will be completed later when his brothers arrive in Egypt during the famine.

TAMAR

After Joseph was sold into slavery, and prior to his being sold to Potiphar, *Genesis* interrupts the flow of the story and inserts this interesting, and seemingly-out-of-place, interlude about Joseph's brother Judah:

Judah had gotten married and had three sons: Er, Onan, and Shelah. When Er came of age, Judah found him a wife named Tamar. But Er was evil (we are not told why), and God took him. After Er died, the tradition of the times was that his brother must marry the widow, and the children of this marriage would be considered the children of the dead elder brother and would continue his line. So Judah had Onan marry Tamar. But Onan wasn't interested in supporting a family that was not considered his own, so when he slept with Tamar he would not ejaculate inside her. This displeased the Lord who had commanded his people to 'be fruitful and multiply', and Onan, too, was taken. Next, Shelah was supposed to marry Tamar, but Shelah was still a boy. So Judah told Tamar to return to her own father, and when Shelah was grown up they would be married.

Shelah grew to manhood, but Judah didn't contact Tamar. She seemed a bit of a jinx, and we can understand that he didn't want to lose his only remaining son.

Long after, Judah's wife passed away. After the period of mourning, he took a trip to Timnah, and Tamar heard that he was going there. She also knew that Judah hadn't done what he promised, for Shelah was obviously now a fully grown man. Since it was her sacred duty to be 'fruitful' and bear children, and she was considered betrothed to the family of Judah and could not marry anyone else, she devised a clever plan:

She took off her widow's garb, covered her face, and sat by the road to Timnah. When Judah saw her, he didn't recognize her and thought that she was a harlot, and he asked to sleep with her. She asked what he would pay. He offered a young sheep. She agreed, but since he didn't have the sheep with him, and was only promising to send it later, she asked for some collateral. Judah gave her his seal, cord and staff. They then slept together and she conceived. He later sent a friend to give her the sheep and retrieve his belongings, but she was nowhere to be found and no one in the region had seen any harlots.

Some months later, Judah received word that Tamar was pregnant. Since she was betrothed to his family, and Shelah hadn't married her, Tamar was evidently guilty of adultery, a capital offense. So Judah ordered her executed. As she was being brought out, she sent a package and a message to her father-in-law: "I am with child by the man to whom these belong. Examine them: whose seal and cord and staff are these?" Judah recognized them and said "She is more righteous than I, inasmuch as I did not give her to my son Shelah."

This public confession of wrongdoing is the *first such confession in the Bible* (long overdue since Adam first blamed Eve and Eve blamed the Serpent), and it is a symbol of profound repentance. Tamar was spared. Thanks to her, Judah has learned to *bear responsibility* and to be *merciful*. Later on, this character preparation will serve him well when he has to confront his brother Joseph. There, as the story of the soul's descent into material life comes to an end, Judah will have to prove to Joseph that he has become a *Tzadik,* a righteous man: and thanks to Tamar, *he is*. Judah will then exemplify the highest form of human love, without which life on earth could never succeed – the willingness to sacrifice one's life for another. This is the final step in the soul's preparation for earthly life.

Of course, after long years in a material body, the soul will become enthralled with the things of the earth, will forget from whence it came, will fall under the thumb of the ego, and will descend into slavery.

Tamar is greatly honored. She gave birth to twins, Perez and Zerah. King David would later be a descendant of Perez, and so too would be the Messiah.

JOCHEBED, MIRIAM, AND BITHIAH

Now we begin the story of the *Greater Mysteries*, the soul's *ascent* from the illusion and slavery of material life back to a state of enlightenment and communion with God. The Hebrew Bible calls this inner journey "the Return to the Promised Land".

Long ago, God had *promised* Abraham that although his descendants (like the *soul*) would descend into material slavery, a time would come in the future when they (i.e., *we*) would be able to return 'home' to Canaan – *back to enlightened communion with God*. But this raises a fairly obvious question: If we started our existence at "home", what was the point of sending us down here just so we can find our way back to where we started? Why did God bother?

One of the clearest answers to this question will come later from Christ, in his 'Parable of the Prodigal Son'. In that story, a father (who represents God) has two sons. The elder son is a very good boy: he always does as he is told, and always remains with his father, helping to take care of the flocks and vineyards. The younger son is rather naughty: he takes his inheritance early, leaves his father's home, and squanders everything in a life of riotous living.

Eventually the younger son 'wakes up' and realizes that he has become a penniless, hungry, hired hand who barely makes a living feeding another man's pigs. He realizes he has reached a bottom, recognizes that he has sinned against his father, and determines to go home where he will beg his father – unworthy though he be – to hire him as a servant and not let him starve.

But when his father sees him coming from a distance, he orders his servants to prepare a great feast, "For this my son was dead, and is alive again! He was lost, and is found!"

When the elder son returns home from the fields, however, and sees what is happening, he becomes very angry and complains bitterly to his father, "This boy, who now returns, wasted everything you gave him on harlots and debauchery. But all these years I have worked for you faithfully, never transgressing, and you have never celebrated with a feast for me!"

It *does* seem a bit unfair. What is Christ trying to tell us?

The elder son represents a child of God who never ventures out into the difficulties of material life. As a result, he has never experienced struggle, failure or sorrow, and he has never experienced triumph, passion or joy. He is 'good', he is innocent, but he can never change or learn or evolve. He has no future, he has no potential, his soul was finished as soon as it began, and as such he is of limited interest and limited use to his father. The younger son goes off into life and falls asleep to his father's world. He is 'bad' and he quickly loses his innocence, he squanders everything and cavorts with harlots, he drinks in all the diverse experiences of earthly life, he feels and laughs and suffers and cries. In the end he realizes he is in a pigsty and makes the decision to begin the journey home.

By the time he gets back, he has evolutionary possibilities that his innocent brother will never know – qualities that are highly treasured by his father. This son was 'dead': his soul, like ours, had descended into the world of illusion. But now, *grown wise with the wisdom of experience, grown strong with a grit that only comes from enduring difficulties and overcoming obstacles,* his soul has returned home to God and is 'alive' again. There is far greater joy in heaven for this accomplishment than for the bland, static existence of his older brother.

We have to experience everything life has to offer and finally get to a place where nothing is left. We have to experience the terrible reality of what the Hindus call *Maya*, what the Buddha called *Suffering*, what the Torah calls *Slavery*. Refusing the full experience of this world of sense, pain, and pleasure, is to reject the plan of God! Spiritual evolution cannot take place until involution is complete and every bit of life has been experienced. Only then can a real choice be made, and we have to make that choice from our own selves.

***

In the land of Egypt the Hebrew slaves were forced to build great cities for Pharaoh, always constrained by their violent and murderous taskmasters, so that their mind, heart and spirit remained dull and empty, and even the wish to escape was nearly forgotten. Like worker ants, they were allowed to exist merely in order to labor for Pharaoh. These great cities and buildings, much like our own, bespoke the narrow worship of the material world and the glorification of human vanity.

But after many years of enslavement, the Israelites were at last crying out to God.

They had greatly multiplied. Pharaoh worried that if a war were to break out with Egypt's neighbors, the thousands of slaves might side with the enemy. So steps had to be taken to reduce their population. Also, Pharaoh had been warned by his astrologers that a child who would free the Hebrews and devastate Egypt was about to be born. So Pharaoh ordered the two Hebrew Midwives, Shiphrah and Puah, to kill all the male babies at birth, but to spare the females: this would stop them from multiplying, but still provide female slaves for the gratification of Egyptian males. This, of course, is a total distortion and perversion of the relations of the sexes, which can only occur under the misguidance of the ego in the realm of illusion.

Shiphrah, according to some stories, was another name for Jochebed, a descendant of the patriarch Levi. Puah was her daughter, also called Miriam. The midwives, who loved and feared God, disobeyed Pharaoh's command, and when called to the palace to explain themselves they boldly made the excuse that Hebrew women were more vigorous than Egyptian women, and would always give birth before the midwives arrived. God blessed the midwives for their courage and devoutness.

49

But Pharaoh then gave a new command, this time to all of his people. "Every boy that is born you shall throw into the Nile, but let every girl live." It is usually assumed that this order referred only to Hebrew children. But some say that Pharaoh's astrologers, who had discerned that this so-called 'redeemer' would meet his demise through water, were unable to discern whether he would be a Hebrew or an Egyptian. Therefore, Pharaoh commanded that all male newborns be thrown into the river.

Jochebed's husband, Amram, an important leader among the Hebrews, met with his council and decided it would be best for the men to live apart from the women, rather than to have children born and then slaughtered by the Egyptians. So he divorced his wife, and the other men followed his example.

But his daughter Miriam reproached him, reminding him that at least Pharaoh's command only applied to males, and who could know whether the edict would even be enforceable. Her father's decision, however, shut the door to life on all Hebrew children and would definitely be enforced. But it was God's Will that the Hebrews 'be fruitful and multiply', and who could say what His divine plan might be or how these events might play out. Amram agreed with the wise words of his daughter, so he went and remarried Jochebed. Again, the other men followed his example.

Jochebed soon conceived a son, and Miriam had a dream which prophesied that this child would be the promised redeemer. Child-killers were watching everywhere, but Jochebed was able to bring her son to birth without being noticed because he was premature and no one was expecting him yet. The Talmud says that when the boy was born the whole house was illuminated with his radiance – for, psychologically, he represented the light of spiritual consciousness entering material consciousness.

His mother was able to hide him for three months, until his birth was expected and prying eyes would be watching. Putting her trust in God, she devised a plan for his survival.

She placed him in an ark and placed it in the Nile to await the will of Providence. Miriam (whose name means 'bitterness' – in part because she could see and empathize with the agony of her people) hid by the river to watch over her baby brother.

Soon the daughter of Pharaoh came with her maid-servants to bathe in the Nile. She heard the cries of the child, saw the basket, and retrieved it. She took pity on him and said, "This must be a Hebrew child", for she could see that he was circumcised. (Some stories say she could even perceive the *Shechinah* who was always beside him and protecting him). Miriam then appeared and convinced Pharaoh's daughter to let her find a Hebrew nurse to suckle the child. She fetched Jochebed. The princess said, "Take this child and nurse it for me, and I will pay your wages." So Jochebed took her son and raised him. Later, when he had grown up, she brought him to Pharaoh's daughter who made him her son. She named him Moses, which means "I drew him out of the water".

And thus Jochebed, whose name means 'Divine Splendor', cared for and raised her son for several years, teaching him to love God, bequeathing to him everything good and useful from Israel, in order to protect him from the negative influences of the Egyptian palace where he would have to go when he was twelve years old. But it is also said in the legends that Pharaoh's daughter, Bithiah, whose name means 'Daughter of God', was an initiate of the Egyptian Mysteries and a devotee of God. She would bequeath to Moses everything that was good and useful from Egypt, and would later join the Israelites in the *Exodus*.

Meanwhile, as soon as the basket was in the river Pharaoh's astrologers discerned through their magical arts that the prophesied redeemer was in the waters of the Nile. They still could not figure out whether he was a Hebrew or an Egyptian (not realizing that he was both), but this no longer mattered. He was in the Nile, they assumed this meant he was destroyed, so they informed Pharaoh and he rescinded the order that all male children were to be killed.

Thus was Moses, who was of both Egypt (Earth) and Israel (Heaven), brought into life, protected, raised, and prepared for his task of redemption (conscious evolution), by a triad of Sacred Feminine power. Without the boldness and wisdom of his sister Miriam, the child would never have been born at all. Without the love of his mother Jochebed, he would never have survived. And without the kindness and piety of his step-mother Bithiah, he would never have fulfilled his destiny.

ZIPPORAH

Moses grew up in Pharaoh's palace, but one day he went out among his own people, became angered at an Egyptian taskmaster whipping a Hebrew slave, killed the Egyptian, and had to run away from a furious Pharaoh. He went to Midian where he met a Priest named Jethro, whose daughter, Zipporah, became Moses' wife.

Years later, after the famous incident at the Burning Bush, when God told him to return to Egypt and free his people, Moses took Zipporah and their two sons and began the journey. And then a very strange thing happened that very first night:

> *At a night encampment on the way,*
> *the Lord encountered him*
> *and sought to kill him.*
> *So Zipporah took a flint and cut off her son's foreskin,*
> *and touched Moses' legs with it, saying,*
> *"You are truly a bridegroom of blood to me!"*
> *And when God let him alone, she added,*
> *"A bridegroom of blood because of the*
> *circumcision." (Exod. 4.24-26)*

A commentary in the Talmud suggests that it was not God Himself who tried to kill Moses in this startling story, but two Angels of Punishment and Destruction that He sent, who came disguised as snakes. They took Moses and swallowed his whole body down to his feet, and only gave him up after Zipporah circumcised her son and touched Moses' feet with the blood.

Here is the customary interpretation: Moses had circumcised one of his sons, but not the other. This was because he was honoring an agreement he had made with his uncircumcised father-in-law, Jethro: Moses had consented to circumcise one child as an Israelite, while the other would remain an uncircumcised Egyptian. But now

Moses had passed beyond the level of Jethro, and this 'agreement' was not acceptable to the Lord.

Others say that God belatedly wished to punish Moses for killing the Egyptian, or that God was still resentful at all the objections Moses had raised at the Burning Bush.

But none of these interpretations have a satisfactory ring to them when compared to the extraordinary bloodiness and eeriness of the story. There has to be more.

God's attempt to kill Moses means that something in Moses, something in the Initiate, has to 'die' and be 'reborn'.

The Talmud adds that there were snakes involved. Snakes, or serpents, symbolize many things, including 'rebirth'. Because of its ability to shed its skin, the serpent is a symbol of rebirth and resurrection: it dives into the earth, eating dust, and signifying death, but it can also rise to the heavens as a phallic symbol, an emblem of life, potency and enlightenment. Here, two vicious serpents try to 'swallow' Moses, trying thereby to bring him back down from his initiatory ascent to the realm of earth and mortality.

Initiation requires a profound inner change – a death and a rebirth. *So God comes to kill him!* It is Zipporah, the sacred inner Feminine, who must protect him and allow the new birth. So Zipporah performs the circumcision and he is 'reborn' by being disgorged by the serpents.

According to Jewish tradition, when a boy is first born he is a child of Adam. Only after circumcision does he become a child of Abraham, and thus a participant in God's covenant. In other words, *circumcision symbolizes a death and rebirth* – a child of Adam dies and is reborn as an Israelite. Later, in *Deuteronomy*, God will speak of the 'circumcision of the heart', and we can see that this symbolism of rebirth refers on a deeper level to the cutting away of the stubborn emotional shell that covers the divine spirit within us and separates us from God. This is the higher meaning of the covenant, the *real* rebirth that is required.

54

It is said in the Kabbalah that circumcision is the way to Heaven, which signifies that spiritual death and rebirth is the way to Heaven. Before leaving Zipporah, we should acknowledge the problem of this Biblical symbolism: literal physical circumcision only relates to males. One explanation for this is that females offer a similar blood sacrifice every month, without any need for an act such as circumcision, giving them a natural and exquisite comprehension of these things which men can only seek to obtain through the performance of imitative rituals. A further explanation is that all the scriptural lessons for 'men' and all the scriptural lessons for 'women' are really directed at the male and female aspects that exist inside each one of us regardless of gender: Moses and Zipporah represent two poles of the soul within *each* of us, and their story takes place within the psyche of both men and women. During the process of spiritual rebirth, this inner act of sacrifice must always be played out. The need to be reborn by 'cutting away the emotional shell that separates us from God' relates to all of us.

The symbolism of this story is magnificent in its symmetry. Consider the implications! The Mind and the Heart, represented by Adam and Eve in the story of the soul's descent, are now represented by Moses and Zipporah in the story of the ascent. Once again, a Serpent, representing the Body, tries to draw the Mind down, which would again invert the soul. This time, however, the woman realizes the appropriate internal relationship, and acknowledges that the Mind, not the Body, is the Heart's true "bridegroom". Thus it is that on the return journey to Enlightenment, the Bible teaches that the Feminine *saves* the soul from a 'Fall'!

If we are going to blame Woman for the 'Fall' in Eden, it's time we gave her full credit for *saving* the soul from a 'Fall' here in Midian.

MIRIAM

O n one particular occasion, during the early years of wandering through the desert, the people demanded that Moses give them water. So God gave Moses the ability to perform a miracle and get water from a rock. Legends say that God did this for the sake of the prophetess Miriam, as a reward for all her merits. The rock became known as "Miriam's Well", and it followed the Israelites throughout their many years of wandering, giving them water until they reached Canaan. This abundant source of nourishment, of course, is an attribute of the Feminine, the *Shechinah*. As we've already noted, the Feminine aspect of Creation is the vehicle, the 'Vessel', through which the Divine can be expressed in this world, and the 'water' she brings forth (from 'stone', i.e., from Matter) is a high level of spiritual Truth.

Miriam has been the personification of the *Shechinah* throughout this part of the story. It is Miriam, the midwife, who brings new life to birth. But eventually we read, *"The Israelites arrived in a body at the wilderness of Zin on the first new moon, and the people stayed at Kadesh ['Holy']. Miriam died there and was buried there."* (Num.20.1)

With her passing, the abundance which she miraculously supplied for the Israelites during their many years in the desert was withdrawn. The rock no longer gave water. As always, the withdrawal of the Mother's nourishment brings a time of suffering. (There is a directly related story in the Greek Myths. There, Demeter is the great Mother, the Sacred Feminine, the goddess of the grain. In the story of the ascent of Demeter and her daughter Persephone back to Olympus, she withdraws this nourishment, causing a famine. In both instances, the symbolism relates to drawing inward, fasting, and preparing oneself for the final ascent.)

A defining characteristic of the Masculine is the need to think things through in a linear, step-by-step manner, to experience a reality that is limited and finite and therefore straightforward, controllable, and 'knowable'. A defining characteristic of the Feminine, on the other hand, is the ability to experience reality in a holistic, open-ended, all-at-once manner, to take in and accept limitlessness and infinity. Needless to say, we each have a share in both of these characteristic abilities. But since *God is endless, infinite, and inherently indefinable and unknowable*, it is the Sacred Feminine in the world (*Women*) and in the individual (the *Heart*) that can get close, and must introduce the Sacred Masculine to the ineffable reality of Divine Being.

This is why Miriam had to die first, before Aaron and Moses. The *Shechinah* must lead the way.

Another defining characteristic of the Masculine is that it expresses the *Active* force within the Creation, and as such it is always involved in doing, fixing, making, and acting. The Feminine, on the other hand, is the *Passive/Receptive* force of Creation. This quality of passivity has been given a very bad name in our frantically productive society, where it's been saddled with negative and destructive connotations of weakness and submission, and we've seen in the story of Adam an example of *irresponsible* passivity – that is, passivity precisely when the male principle *ought* to be *active*. But if the truth be told, passivity is the higher quality. *Action* is the emblem of the realm of Matter: the Masculine 'does'. *Passivity* is the emblem of the realm of Spirit: the Feminine 'is'.

It is precisely this ability to be passive, to 'be' without having to 'do', that allows the Sacred Feminine Vessel to receive pure, endless, unknowable Being, without having to limit it or define it through any agenda of her own, and then to bring it to birth as infinite abundance and love in the physical world.

This is also why, in the Greek myths, the 'Terrestrial Aphrodite' had the task of binding souls into bodies and sending them down to the Earth, and the 'Celestial

Aphrodite' had the task of *un*binding evolved souls *from* their bodies and *releasing them into bliss*. Only the Feminine power in the world can do these things.

RAHAB

Not long after Miriam's death, Aaron passed away. Moses soon named Joshua as his successor, and then he, too, passed on. (The name "Joshua" means "God is the Savior". It is the same name that will later be translated in the New Testament as "Jesus").

The soul's journey is coming to an end. Just before Joshua and the Israelites enter the Promised Land, Joshua sends two spies on a reconnaissance mission. The spies set out for Jericho, according to the Bible, *"and they came to the house of a harlot named Rahab and lodged there."*

Now why, of all places, would Joshua's spies go to the house of a harlot? Doesn't the Bible say that God *hates* harlots?

God does not hate anyone. A 'harlot' *symbolizes the seductive sensations* and desires that inflame our lower nature but leave the soul unsatisfied. The name 'Rahab' means *proud* or *arrogant*, and it is a term that is sometimes used to signify the material domain of 'Egypt'. Jericho, Rahab's city, means *Moon* – which is another symbol for the illusory level of life that 'Egypt' also represents. The soul's first mission in the Promised Land will be to once and for all completely destroy 'Jericho', so that no illusions or attachments remain and the soul can reach enlightenment.

But 'Rahab' means something else as well. Rahab symbolizes the primordial *Chaos* that was 'vanquished by the Creator' in Hebrew legends. For example, *Isaiah* will later say: *"It was You that hacked Rahab in pieces, That pierced the Dragon. It was You that dried up the Sea, The waters of the great deep."* And *Job* will say: *"By His power He stilled the sea; By His skill He struck down Rahab"*. The Greeks will later tell the same story. In their version, the first goddess, Gaia, the transcendent Mother-principle, is *Chaos*. The first god, Uranos, who represents the *Light of Reason,* stills the turbulent waters and brings *Order* to Chaos.

According to another legend from the oral tradition in the Talmud and Kabbalah, Joshua was swallowed by a 'sea-monster' in his infancy, but at a distant point of the sea-coast the monster spewed him forth unharmed. So on a deep psychological level, we can see that Rahab was the sea-monster who spewed forth Joshua – in mythical terms, his 'mother'. Later on, according to the legends, Joshua will *marry* Rahab (in her current incarnation as the 'harlot of Jericho'), so she is also his 'wife'. This is a recurrent theme in scripture and mythology. Eve was Adam's wife, but she was also his Mother – since he calls her 'the Mother of all Living'. In Greek mythology, some stories have Gaia as Uranos' wife, while in other stories she's his mother. The Sacred Masculine and the Sacred Feminine are *wed* in the 'Above' (prior to separation into the sexes). But for the Masculine to enter this world 'Below', he must come to birth *through* the Feminine and thereby become her *son.*

Like the Greek Gaia, Rahab is the ancient archetype that underlies the power of the Sacred Feminine. The Feminine power in the scriptures is not some soft, sweet, gentle child, representing all the 'nice' qualities that are missing in men. She is the *Shechinah*, the 'Presence' of God in the Creation, the force that hovers over the Ark of the Covenant, the 'Mother of All Living' who pours forth all the forms and qualities in the infinite universe. She is *Chaos,* the turbulent passions. She is the Beauty of Rachel and the Wisdom of Leah. She is Miriam's prophetic power. She embodies the mysteries of blood, sex, birth, and death. She is the Sea, the boundless power of the Unconscious. She is the Mother and the Whore and the Wife and the Destroyer. In Jericho, she lives in a great tower, high above the city. Rahab was said to be the most beautiful woman in the world, a theme we have seen before when a woman in the story represents the Sacred Feminine.

As always, the Masculine needs her protection, so when the king of Jericho heard rumors of spies, Rahab hid the two men on her roof and convinced the king to take his soldiers out of the city and search for them in the nearby hills. Then she made a deal with the men that when the day of Jericho's destruction came, they would first come and rescue her and her family. The spies of course agreed. This is the end of the story in the Hebrew Bible, and now, as the soul begins its final battle and ascends to Enlightenment, Rahab, the Sacred Feminine, must reunite with Joshua, the Sacred Masculine, so that together they can merge back into Oneness and return home to God. The *Shechinah* was present at the beginning of Creation, she imbues all levels of Creation from the lowest to the highest, and she is still present here at the end of the story waiting for the Masculine to return. Just before the final destruction of Jericho, Rahab, the rescuer who saved the spies, is rescued in return, and she returns to Israel where the Bible says, "she continues to dwell to this very day."

THE VIRGIN MARY

W̶e now move on to the story as it is told in the Gospels.
It's always the same inner story: the quest for the soul's illumination. The ancient Greeks presented their Wisdom Teaching through stories of dreamlike gods and goddesses who personified the powers of Nature and Divinity, as well as their own inner archetypes and spiritual attributes. The Hebrews presented their Wisdom Teaching through adventures and legends that they wove around their ancestors. Now we will see that Christianity presents its Wisdom Teaching through the extraordinary story of one divine man, Jesus of Nazareth, who single-handedly traversed all the levels of Being in one lifetime, as he and his disciples played out the entire drama of Initiation on the stage of world history, and everyone was, and is, invited to watch and participate.

The Greek word *pleroo*, which is translated as 'fulfill', has nothing to do with 'making predictions come true'. It means to make something perfect, to give back what is lacking, so that it overflows with truth and goodness. To say that Jesus 'fulfilled the Scriptures' does *not* mean that the Hebrew Bible was somehow 'really' about him. It isn't. *It means that he did everything the Scriptures symbolically instruct us to do*: he publicly performed and fully achieved all the steps of Initiation, perfectly demonstrating the inner psychological and spiritual meaning of everything that is revealed in the Hebrew Bible.

But Christ did do something new, something that makes his teaching different from anything that had come before and would bring about an enormous change in the level of consciousness of humanity. The Mysteries had always been for the chosen few. The specific details of rites and ceremonies that took place during an actual Initiation had always been a closely guarded secret, hidden in symbolism, hidden in secret ceremonies, hidden in the mists of time. The idea had always been that it was dangerous for uninitiated people to have too much knowledge which they were not prepared to digest, since this could only lead to confusion and resentment.

Christ would not disagree. But he was determined to let everyone share in at least *some* of the fruits of the Mysteries, if only in a small way. He could not give everyone the entire experience, nor would he have wanted to. But he wanted everyone to know, with absolute certainty, as a *result of their own experience* and what they *witnessed with their own eyes*, that the Truths of the Mysteries definitely existed, that there were higher levels of Being which every human being had a right to, and which they would one day be able to attain.

It was time for the sacred wisdom that had always been scrupulously concealed to flow directly into history and become the possession of all humanity. So he performed the entire Mystery Play on the stage of world history, and instead of swearing his disciples to secrecy, he sent them forth with orders to shine their light before others, so that everyone could see.

***

Woman provides the passageway into life. This of course is true literally, but this literal truth is a material reflection of an even deeper spiritual truth. As we discussed in the story of Miriam, it is through the Sacred Feminine that the soul enters the material world, and it is only through her intercession that the evolved and perfected soul can return home to God.

In the New Testament, the name 'Miriam' is translated as *Mary*. In the Gospels, *Mary* represents the *Shechinah* – God's "Presence" in this world. As the story begins, Mary is betrothed, but not yet married, to a man named Joseph. According to the story, she was a 'virgin'. This is actually a mistranslation: the word translated as 'virgin' only means 'a young woman of marriageable age'. However, we need not quarrel with the use of the word 'virgin' if it is taken in its symbolic sense: to say that Mary was a 'virgin' means that her soul was pure and completely free of sin. This state of being is not brought about by avoiding sexual behavior. It is brought about by *inner spiritual effort*. The Gospel is simply acknowledging the extraordinarily level of holiness that she had attained – a degree of spiritual perfection that was so high and sacred that her soul, by itself, could conceive and give birth to Divinity.

As the story unfolds we are told surprisingly little about Jesus' mother. But she is present at the three most critical moments of Jesus' life: his birth, his first miracle (which she asks him to perform and which inaugurates his mission), and his death.

The first miracle takes place at Cana. Jesus is attending a marriage, and Mary is also there. The Sacrament of Marriage symbolizes the re-unification of the earthly level of the soul with the heavenly level of the soul, the 'raising up' of our lower aspects: in other words, the internal "Marriage of Heaven and Earth". At *this* wedding, according to the Gospel of John, the wine being served to the guests ran out, and Mary said to Jesus: *"They have no wine." And Jesus said to her, "Woman, what concern is that to you and to me? My hour has not yet come." His mother said to the servants, "Do whatever he tells you." Now standing there were six stone water jars for the Jewish rites of purification, each holding twenty or thirty gallons. Jesus said to them, "Fill up the jars with water." And they filled them up to the brim. "Now draw some out and take it to the chief steward." So they took it out.... [The water] had become wine.*

Jesus had just said that the lack of wine was no concern of his, since his 'hour' had 'not yet come'. But a moment later he turned six jars of water into wine. What happened in the interim that caused him to change his mind?

Well, *this* is what happened: *His mother said to the servants, "Do whatever he tells you."*

Now remember our premise that the Gospel story gives us a representation of the steps of a spiritual initiation. The "Marriage at Cana" indicates that the soul is now rising to the 'heavenly' level. The Divine Mother is the ruler of this level, just as the Sun is the ruler of the Planets. The soul, represented by Jesus as he performs the initiatory rites for all of us to watch, is destined to rule this realm as well, *but he cannot assume this authority until he is commissioned by the Mother.* But something is lacking. Without wine, evidently, the Sacred Marriage of Heaven and Earth cannot proceed. Even though Jesus objects that his hour has not yet come, Mary decides that he *is* ready and she gives him her authority: "Whatever he tells you," she said to her subjects, "you must do." Jesus then made sure there would be abundant wine.

Let's look more closely at what this symbolism means.

We've seen that *Water* is a symbol of God's Truth, which rains down upon the Earth. At our level of Being, this high level of Truth must be filtered through *stone*, which represents a *literal* level of truth, so that we can comprehend it with our sense-based consciousness. When God gave Moses the Ten Commandments, for instance, the divine *words* had to be inscribed on tablets of *stone*. This is a similar image to the water that Jesus now has the servants pour into jars made of stone. But the Tablets were being prepared for people who were still at the beginning of their initiatory journey. Here, at the level of the Sacred Marriage, Truth can blend with the initiate's *higher* level of Being (instead of with 'stone') and be transformed into spiritual *Wisdom* (even *better* than Truth, far beyond the confines of material sensation or even abstract reasoning.). This merging and coalescing of Truth with higher Being abolishes the illusory dualism between 'I' and 'World', and the Initiate begins to directly 'see' actual sacred Reality. The attainment of this high level of *consciousness,* the opening if the Inner Eye, is the mystical meaning of the transformation of *Water* into *Wine*

Jesus could not do this until Mary determined that he was ready and allowed it, another demonstration of how our soul can only return to God through the intercession of the Sacred Feminine.

THE SAMARITAN WOMAN

In the Gospel of *John*, Jesus comes to 'Jacob's Well' where Jacob had met Rachel. But this time a high representative of the Feminine doesn't appear. Instead, a *lower* representative appears, a Samaritan woman who doesn't recognize Christ (though she's heard he's coming and hopes to see him). She draws some water and Jesus asks for a drink. She's surprised, since Jews did not share things with Samaritans. Jesus says, "If you knew who is saying, 'Give me a drink,' you would have asked *him*, and he would have given you *living* water."

But this is the *lower* Feminine principle, and she gives herself away with a literal and superficial question: "Sir, you have no bucket and the well is deep. Where do you get that living water?" Jesus answers "Everyone who drinks of *this* water will be thirsty again, but those who drink of the water *I* give them will *never* be thirsty."

She still doesn't understand, and responds somewhat comically, "Sir, give me *this* water, so I may never be thirsty or have to keep coming here to draw water." Jesus, perhaps a bit exasperated, tells her to "Go, call your husband, and come back." At first, this seems an odd bit of chauvinism, but he's speaking symbolically and what this means is that her consciousness is completely attuned to her lower physical nature, which is *why* she understands everything *literally*, and he wants her to turn to her higher Mind, her proper 'husband'. But she says, "I have no husband." "You're right", he says, "for you have had five husbands, and the one you have now is not your husband." The five husbands are her five senses, none of which is appropriate.

Slowly, she begins to get a little clearer. She still can't *'see'* very well, but she *wants* to -- and this means she eventually *will*. "I know the Messiah is coming", she says. And Jesus says, "I am he, the one who is speaking to you." At this point, the disciples appear. *John* tells us they were "astonished that he was speaking with a woman", but they wisely kept their mouths shut. The Samaritan woman then left and went back to her village, where she told everyone about Jesus and asked them whether *they* thought he could be the Messiah. We're told that "many believed in him *because of the woman's testimony.*" Then they "left the city" and went to meet him.

Meanwhile, the text says that Jesus' own disciples had gone "*to* the city" in search of food – in other words, they had gone off in the opposite direction, *away* from Christ, seeking sustenance in the lower realm, in Samaria, while the residents of Samaria were ironically coming *upward,* searching for sustenance *in Christ.* Now the disciples have returned and they urge Jesus to eat. But he says he has *other* food, food they know nothing about. Like the Samaritan woman, they take this literally and ask each other, 'who gave him food?' Jesus patiently tries to explain, "My food is to do the will of him who sent me and to complete his work." He then tells them not to think that someday 'in the future' the harvest will be ready. The harvest of *this* food is *here now.* Open your 'eyes', he says, "and see how the fields are ripe for harvesting."

At this point the Samaritans arrive and ask him to spend time with them, and Jesus "stayed there two days". After this experience they said to the woman, "it is no longer because of what you *said* that we believe, for we have heard for *ourselves,* and we *know* that this is truly the Savior of the world."

This is a major point that the Bible often makes but no one seems to hear it! Faith is *not* 'believing what someone else tells us'. Belief is simply adhering to one conviction or another on thoughtless and inadequate grounds: perhaps because someone told us to believe it, perhaps because believing it makes us happy or comfortable, perhaps because it spares us the effort of thinking for ourselves. Faith, on the other hand, is the result of one's own authentic experience of the reality of God. Faith is *knowing,* with absolute *certainty,* for oneself, from *one's own inner efforts and experience.*

THE WOMAN WITH THE ALABASTER JAR

In *Luke's* gospel a Pharisee invites Jesus to dinner. *Luke* uses the word "Pharisee" to represent narrow-minded religious bigots, in all times and places, who have lost sight of the inner spiritual *meaning* of religious rules and customs. The word also applies to that place *in ourselves* that does this.

> *And a woman in the city, who was a sinner, having*
> *learned that he was eating in the Pharisee's house,*
> *brought an alabaster jar of ointment.*
> *She stood behind him at his feet, weeping, and began to*
> *bathe his feet with the tears and to dry them*
> *with her hair. Then she continued kissing his feet and*
> *anointing them with the ointment.*

Here we have a virtual fountain of priceless symbolism. Women of the Middle East would often carry ointments, oils and perfumes in alabaster jars, and this is not the only time that Jesus will be anointed by a woman who uses a fragrant balm that she keeps in an alabaster jar. Anointing, as well as bathing one's feet and kissing, were common signs of hospitality at this time. But in this case, these customary gestures are performed with an *un*customary extravagance.

'Anointing with oil' is a Biblical symbol for the 'fire' of the Holy Spirit entering the soul of the initiate (because oil is the *fuel* of fire). In fact, the word *Messiah* means 'the anointed one'. Anointing the *head* with oil is a symbol for confirming, clearing, and strengthening the Mind, and it is the ritual which many ancient traditions, including Judaism, have used to empower a King. In many traditional mythologies, this anointing would be done by a woman, the *bride* of the king.

But in this story, it is the *feet* that are anointed. 'Feet' symbolize the foundation of our physical life, but through the act of *walking* they also symbolize the soul's efforts to

71

advance. 'Tears' are a symbol of the soul's suffering in the pursuit of divine Truth, its remorse when looking squarely at its bondage to external life, and its compassion for those who remain asleep and enslaved. 'Hair' sits at the apex of the Mind, and is a symbol of the highest qualities of the physical realm reaching upwards to touch God. A woman's hair in particular is a symbol of the pure feminine receptivity which alone allows divinity to enter the world. Lastly, a 'kiss' symbolizes love and union, such as the 'kiss of heaven and earth' as well as the kiss of two human lovers.

Naturally, this woman with the alabaster jar was a sinner (a word which actually only means "*missing the mark*", that we have set, or ought to set, for *ourselves*), just as we *all* are sinners at our level of Being – mistaking the illusory for the real, worshipping wealth and fame (the Bible calls this *idolatry*), and doing anything necessary to achieve them (the Bible calls this *harlotry*). She, however, has changed. But the Pharisee *within* us, the hypocrite who swells with pride while observing empty religious formalism, who obeys rules technically but not spiritually, and who constantly worries about how he appears in other people's eyes, could only feel disgust and say to himself, "If this man were a prophet, he would have known who and what kind of woman this is who is touching him – that she is a sinner." Jesus, of course, heard what was in his heart, and he said to the Pharisee: "*I entered your house; you gave me no water for my feet, but she bathed my feet with her tears and dried them with her hair. You gave me no kiss, but from the time I came in she has not stopped kissing my feet. You did not anoint my head with oil, but she has anointed my feet with ointment.*"

All of this demonstrates quite clearly, Jesus continues, that this is a woman who is full of love, a woman who "*loves much*". Both Jesus and Moses tell us that 'love of neighbor and love of God' *summarize all esoteric teaching*. The necessary karmic response here is that her many sins have been forgiven. The Pharisee, on the other hand, has loved but little, and thus his sins have *not* been forgiven.

In the metaphysical sequence of the inner story, the Initiate's soul has now been given lessons in *Hope* (the Mysteries and all that they promise are hereafter in the possession of everyone – stone can turn into water, and water can turn into wine), *Faith* ('Believing' is inadequate for the Sacred Quest, but 'Faith' is *certainty* earned by one's own experience), and *Love* (which summarizes all true spiritual teaching). It is almost time for the Sacred Feminine to merge with the Sacred Masculine.

MARY AND MARTHA

In the Hebrew Bible, the Lord has Moses tell the people that upon returning to the Promised Land all animal offerings and sacrifices are to be accompanied with meal offerings, oil, and wine. The symbolic meaning is that the Initiate, upon entering the divine realm, will have to be in a state of perfect wholeness and completeness – body (*bread*), mind (*oil*), and heart (*wine*).

In this parallel moment in Christ's initiatory journey (he will soon ascend the Cross and return to Heaven), he enters "a certain village, where a woman named Martha welcomed him into her home. She had a sister named Mary, who sat at the Lord's feet and listened to what he was saying."

> *But Martha was distracted by her many*
> *tasks; so she came to him and asked,*
> *"Lord, do you not care that my sister has*
> *left me to do all the work by myself?*
> *Tell her then to help me."*
> *But the Lord answered her, "Martha,*
> *Martha, you are worried and distracted*
> *by many things; there is need of only one*
> *thing. Mary has chosen the better part,*
> *which will not be taken away from her.*
> *(Luke.10.40-42)*

Martha represents the *Active* side of life, the exoteric side, the *Body* – 'bread'. Her sister Mary represents the *Contemplative* side of life, the esoteric side, the *Heart* – water that has been turned into 'wine'. Christ himself is the 'oil', the fire of the Spirit that descends into the higher *Mind.*

Christ teaches, Martha serves, and Mary listens receptively to the higher Mind. This is an image of the three elements of our soul in their proper relationship. Even here, the 'serpent' tries to draw 'Eve' downward ("Tell her to help me!"). But Christ tells Martha that Mary is *not supposed* to be distracted by the shattered fragments in the lower world. Mary has chosen the "better part" (the esoteric over the exoteric), and "it will not be taken away from her." This is precisely the state of holiness which the initiate must attain in order to enter heaven.

***

Later in the story we are told:

> *Now a certain man was ill,*
> *Lazarus of Bethany,*
> *the village of Mary and her sister Martha....*
> *So the sisters sent a message to Jesus,*
> *"Lord, he whom you love is ill."*
> *But when Jesus heard it, he said,*
> *This illness does not lead to death;*
> *rather it is for God's glory,*
> *so that the Son of God*
> *may be glorified through it."*
> *(John.11.1-4)*

The name 'Lazarus' means *assistance of God*, which tells us that Lazarus is able to help manifest God's plan. Jesus waited two days, and then told his disciples that they were going back to Judea. The disciples were worried, for they knew there were Jews in Judea (in the Gospels, 'Jews' – other than Jesus himself and his disciples – represent our inner tendencies toward literalism, just as 'Egyptians' did in the Hebrew stories) who were ready to 'stone' Jesus (that is, drag him down to the material state of being). Nonetheless, he said:

> *Our friend Lazarus has fallen asleep,*
> *but I am going there to awaken him.*
> *(John.11.11)*

When Jesus arrived in Bethany, Lazarus had been in the tomb for four days. Many Jews had come from Jerusalem and were also there, consoling Mary and Martha.

"When Martha heard that Jesus was coming, she went and met him, while Mary stayed at home" – the *Active* element went to meet him, but the *Contemplative* element remained silently within. Martha said, "Lord, if you had been here, my brother would not have died. But even now I know that God will give you whatever you ask of him." Jesus was surprised by these comments, and said, "Your brother will rise again." Martha replied, "I know that he will rise again in the resurrection on the last day." But that is not what Jesus meant. So he tried again.: "*I am* the resurrection and the life."

Those who believe in me,
even though they die, will live,
and everyone who lives and believes in me
will never die.
Do you believe this?
(John.11.26)

Martha responded by saying, "Yes, Lord. I believe that you are the Messiah, the Son of God, the one coming into the world." But again, she has not understood. She says she believes in *him*, but that is not what he really asked her. She believes her brother is dead, though Jesus has just told her that he is *not* dead. And leaving it at that, she "went back and called her sister Mary, and told her privately, 'The Teacher is here and is calling for you.'"

When Mary heard this, "she got up quickly and went to him." Many of the Jews who were in the house followed her, thinking she was going to the grave and intending to console her.

When she came to Jesus, "she knelt at his feet and said to him, 'Lord, if you had been here, my brother would not have died.'" The same comment! A little different, perhaps: she did not follow it up with Martha's second statement, and unlike Martha "she knelt at his feet." But it still reveals a certain lack of faith. If the sisters understood that everyone who "believes in me will never die", why were they so distraught?

> *When Jesus saw her weeping,*
> *and the Jews who came with her also*
> *weeping, he was greatly disturbed in spirit*
> *and deeply moved. (John.11.33)*

Other translations say he was "deeply moved in spirit, and troubled himself", or "he groaned in spirit and was troubled." But none of these do justice to the actual meaning of the original Greek text. Jesus was not 'disturbed' and 'troubled'. Jesus was *angry*, and *deeply disappointed*.

He then asked, "Where have you laid him?" They said, "Lord, come and see." And then a most remarkable thing is recorded in *John.11.35*.

> *Jesus wept.*

When the Jews saw him weeping, some of them said, "See how he loved him!" Others added, "Could not he who opened the eyes of the blind man have kept this man from dying?"

But Jesus was not weeping because his dear friend Lazarus had died. How absurd would that be?! He wept at the realization that they still did not understand, they still did not have complete faith, they still did not trust in the Father. He wept because they were still so miserable and unhappy and attached to the life of this world, and they could not see that it was only an illusion and Lazarus was not dead in Eternity. He would have to *show* them, he would have to give them 'proof', but it made him weep. And as he wept, his tears watered the earth – symbolic of Christ's higher Truth descending and imbuing the world.

This is a wonderful symmetrical moment. When Abraham was *leaving* the Promised Land, Sarah displayed a small amount of *doubt* – she did not really believe God's promise that she would have a son, Isaac, at her advanced age. Now, as the 'Son' is almost ready to *return* to the 'Promised Land', this small amount of doubt, here displayed by Mary, has to be healed once and for all.

He walked to the tomb. It was a cave, with a great stone lying against it, a symbol of the massive inertia of material illusion blocking the Divine. "Take away the stone," he ordered. Martha fretted and said, "Lord, already there is a stench because he has been dead four days." But Jesus sternly replied, "Did I not tell you that if you believed, you would see the glory of God?" So she backed away and they took away the stone.

> *The dead man came out, his hands and feet*
> *bound with strips of cloth, and his face*
> *wrapped in a cloth. Jesus said to them,*
> *"Unbind him, and let him go." (John.11.43-44)*

MARY MAGDALENE

Shortly after the scenes with the Samaritan woman and the woman with the alabaster Jar, the *high* Feminine appeared at last in the guise of an abundance of women led by a triad of Power, Grace and Joy, reuniting with the Sacred Masculine so that together they would be able to complete the journey back to Divinity.

> *Soon afterwards, he went on through cities and villages, proclaiming and bringing the good news of the kingdom of God. The twelve were with him, as well as some women who had been cured of evil spirits and infirmities: Mary, called Magdalene ['Greatness' or 'High Tower'] from whom seven demons had gone out, and Joanna ['Grace']the wife of Herod's steward Chuza, and Susanna ['Joy'], and many others, who provided for them out of their resources. (Luke.8.1-3)*

To say that these women "provided for them out of their resources" is an example of something we have seen many times since the story of Abraham and Sarah: the Sacred Feminine taking care of the Masculine. But let's talk more specifically about Mary Magdalene. To say that Mary had been 'cured of seven demons' does not mean, as has often been suggested, that she was a particularly egregious sinner. She was no more a sinner than you or I. But *Mary has been fully initiated.*

The highly symbolic number 'Seven' signifies *every level of a complete process*: a passage through seven stages is an ancient and universal symbol of complete achievement. Thus, we have seven days of creation, seven colors of the spectrum, and seven notes in the musical scale. The Hindus speak of seven chakras, Aristotle speaks of seven spheres, Dante speaks of seven heavens. There are even seven deadly sins. To say that Mary was 'cured of seven demons' means that *every level of Mary Magdalene had been purified and perfected.* She is the archetype of the soul that drinks in the total experience of life on earth, who has the good sense and humility to ask for God's help (like the Samaritan woman), who pours forth love and attains complete forgiveness (like the woman with the alabaster jar), who completes all of the Great Work and has been healed at every level of her soul. She will now remain the powerful ally and protectress of the Spirit right to the very end – Mary, unlike the other apostles, *will still be present at the Cross.* And apart from Jesus himself, there is no indication that anyone else in the New Testament achieves her level of initiation, with the single exception of her male-counterpart, Lazarus.

Was Mary Magdalene the secret wife of Jesus? Was she the 'vessel' of his semen and his children, the mother of a lost line of kings, and thus the authentic 'Holy Grail'?

Metaphorically, Jesus and Mary, like Joshua and Rahab, have *always* been 'wed'. In the New Testament the Sacred Feminine is always called 'Mary' – and once again, as is always the case, 'Mary' is *both* Jesus' Mother and his Wife.

In terms of literal history, however, all of this is beside the point. Not because it is unimportant to return the Sacred Feminine to her rightful place in western civilization. On the contrary*, it is urgent.* But chasing after gossip, scandal, and conspiracy theories, is not the way to do it.

We have to stop reducing the vast meaning and awesome power of symbolism and mythology to mere questions of literal fact or fiction. Were they 'really' married? Perhaps. But if we found a Marriage Certificate with Jesus' and Mary's signatures buried in a desert cave, how would this discovery contribute anything to the perfection of one's soul? The search for this kind of 'proof' is fascinating and fun, but it is of no spiritual significance. It is merely a diversion from real spiritual work.

The reason we must restore the Sacred Feminine to her full divine stature in our lives and culture is because without her all spiritual evolution is *impossible*! Without her all the ancient myths and holy scriptures are *useless*! We cannot follow Demeter and Persephone back to Olympus, we cannot obey the Law of Moses, we cannot walk in Christ's footsteps, if we continue to misconstrue everything that is said about the perfect equality, the required harmony, and the absolute inter-dependence of 'Male' and 'Female' at every level of Creation. All of this is in the stories. Nothing is hidden. But the meaning of the words has to be penetrated and understood. As we saw in the stories of Miriam and the Virgin Mary, *only the Sacred Feminine, within the soul of a human being or the soul of a civilization, can receive the pure, endless, unknowable Being of God, without trying to limit it or define it, and then bring it to birth as infinite abundance and love in this world. And only the Sacred Feminine, through pure noetic intuition, can reconnect us to that infinite, timeless, Divine Being, and lead us home. She is the key to Creation and Return.*

The consequences of her degradation, a crime for which men and women are equally responsible, are constantly and painfully visible in the disintegration of compassion, decency, and human meaning that we witness all around us.

PEACE ON EARTH

GOODWILL TOWARD ALL MEN, WOMEN AND
ESPECIALLY CHILDREN

AND ALL THAT LIVES AND BREATHES

ABOUT THE AUTHOR

Dr. Andrew Cort is an author, speaker, teacher, attorney, and doctor of chiropractic. He received his BA and MA from Colgate University, his Doctor of Chiropractic Degree from New York Chiropractic College, and his Law Degree from Boston College Law School.

In addition to academic studies in literature, science, law, and mathematics, he has studied the work of many spiritual traditions – from the Bible, Plato, the Qur'an, Dante, and many others, to contemporary teachers including G.I. Gurdjieff, P.D. Ouspensky, Rudolf Steiner, Paul Brunton, Anthony Damiani, Oscar Ichazo, and Sri Aurobindo.

His writings and seminars encompass Spirituality, Interfaith Religion, Science, Mythology, Education, Healing, and how these all interact with each other and with contemporary culture.

Please visit Dr. Cort's Website at
www.AndrewCort.com
and his Blog
INTERFAITH AWAKENING
www.InterfaithAwakening.com
(A Blog About Compassion, Unity, Wisdom, Peace, and Spiritual Enlightenment, for all Faiths, all Traditions, and all Cultures)

Andrew Cort lives in Woodstock, NY. He is available for Talks and Seminars and can be contacted at
Andrew@AndrewCort.com

Made in the USA
Middletown, DE
22 April 2015